Poicephalus Parrots

Poicephalus Parrots As Pets

Poicephalus Parrot Facts & Information, where to buy, health, diet, lifespan, types, breeding, fun facts and more!

By: Lolly Brown

Copyrights and Trademarks

All rights reserved. No part of this book may be reproduced or transformed in any form or by any means, graphic, electronic, or mechanical, including photocopying, recording, taping, or by any information storage retrieval system, without the written permission of the author.

This publication is Copyright ©2019 NRB Publishing, an imprint. Nevada. All products, graphics, publications, software and services mentioned and recommended in this publication are protected by trademarks. In such instance, all trademarks & copyright belong to the respective owners. For information consult www.NRBpublishing.com

Disclaimer and Legal Notice

This product is not legal, medical, or accounting advice and should not be interpreted in that manner. You need to do your own due-diligence to determine if the content of this product is right for you. While every attempt has been made to verify the information shared in this publication, neither the author, neither publisher, nor the affiliates assume any responsibility for errors, omissions or contrary interpretation of the subject matter herein. Any perceived slights to any specific person(s) or organization(s) are purely unintentional.

We have no control over the nature, content and availability of the web sites listed in this book. The inclusion of any web site links does not necessarily imply a recommendation or endorse the views expressed within them. We take no responsibility for, and will not be liable for, the websites being temporarily unavailable or being removed from the internet.

The accuracy and completeness of information provided herein and opinions stated herein are not guaranteed or warranted to produce any particular results, and the advice and strategies, contained herein may not be suitable for every individual. Neither the author nor the publisher shall be liable for any loss incurred as a consequence of the use and application, directly or indirectly, of any information presented in this work. This publication is designed to provide information in regard to the subject matter covered.

Neither the author nor the publisher assume any responsibility for any errors or omissions, nor do they represent or warrant that the ideas, information, actions, plans, suggestions contained in this book is in all cases accurate. It is the reader's responsibility to find advice before putting anything written in this book into practice. The information in this book is not intended to serve as legal, medical, or accounting advice.

Foreword

One of the most popular and friendliest types of bird is the Poicephalus Parrots. They've originated from Africa just like the African Grey Parrots. There are various types of species in the Poicephalus family; one of the most famous species of poicephalus birds is the Senegal parrot which is a good choice if you're a first time bird keeper. In general, Poicephalus birds are easy going, and loving pets. They're not particularly loud, and they can slightly mimic sounds but not quite the same level as the African Greys.

Poicephalus parrots and most pet parrots in general are not that easy to take care of as with any other pets. Just like African Greys, these parrots will need adequate cages, a source of stimulation like toys (though they are not as destructive compared to other bird species), and of course, time and attention from his/ her owners.

Keeping these birds shouldn't be just for the sake of having a pet companion or for the sake of just taking care of them; you need to be committed when it comes to various pet – related tasks, and you need to have enough knowledge on how to properly raise them. In this book you'll learn general information about poicephalus birds, the different types of species under their family, and how you can become a great bird keeper!

Table of Contents

Introduction 1

Chapter One: Poicephalus Parrots in General 2

    Biological Information 3

    Diet of Poicephalus Species 5

    Potential Behavioral Problems 5

    Behavioral Changes in Relation to Sexual Maturity 7

    Distribution and Habitat in the Wild 9

    Threats and Conservation Status 11

Chapter Two: Poicephalus Species and 14

Sub - Species 14

Chapter Three: Acquiring, Feeding and Housing Poicephalus Parrots 28

    Benefits of Acquiring Poicephalus Parrots from Hobbyists 29

    Benefits of Adopting from Rescue Centers 31

    Searching for an Avian Veterinarian 33

    Micro – chipping Your Poicephalus 34

        Cage Essentials and House Set - Up 36

        Other Parrot Essentials 41

    Housebreaking Your Poicephalus Parrot 43

    Feeding Your Poicephalus Parrots 47

Recommended Food Brands 52

Hand – Feeding Your Parrot 71

Chapter Four: Grooming Tips for Your Poicephalus Parrots 74

Grooming Your Poicephalus Parrots 75

Cleaning Your Parrot.. 76

Clipping the Wings... 77

Keeping the Beak Healthy 79

Trimming the Nails... 80

Chapter Five: Forming a Bond with Your Poicephalus Parrots... 82

Tips in Gaining Your Bird's Trust 83

Handling Proper 87

Training Proper 89

Taming Your Poicephalus Parrot 92

Chapter Six: Pairing Poicephalus... 96

Bonded Pairs vs. Compatible Pairs 97

Courting and Mating.. 99

Egg Laying and Nesting... 100

Nesting and Territorial Issues.. 100

Signs of Sexual Maturity 102

Chapter Seven: Raising Poicephalus Chicks........................ 104

Parenting 105

Pulling Chicks 107

Sibling Aggression 107

Glossary of Important Terms 110

Photo Credits 116

References 117

Introduction

Poicephalus is a Greek word which means "made of head." They are small to medium – sized birds, and their body structure is quite stocky. They are short in stature, have large heads and beaks as well as square tails. The genus of Poicephalus has a lot of sub - species that are native in the regions of Africa particularly in Senegal, Ethiopia, and South Africa. They are usually distributed in sub – Saharan regions, and tropical areas. The most common types of Poicephalus species that are kept as pets include Senegal, Jardines (brown/ red – headed), Red – Bellied, and Meyer's

Introduction

parrot. The largest species of the Poicephalus family is the Cape Parrot.

The average size of these parrots is around 8 to 10 inches in length; their pint – sized stocky bodies, and fun attitude are the reasons why they are slightly advantageous to keep as pets over their bigger cousins like the African Grey birds and Amazon parrots. The plumage of Poicephalus species are not flashy compared to their other African native cousins but the combination of green and yellow body colored is what makes them appealing and unique. Most poicephalus species are adequately suited for average sized parrot enclosures that can fit inside your home, or you can also house them in outdoor aviaries to provide for an extra room especially if you're planning to keep two birds or more.

When it comes to sexual dimorphism, some poicephalus birds can be identified visually while other are not sexually dimorphic – if you happen to get a poicephalus species that are not sexually dimorphic, you'll need to have your bird's DNA tested so that you can tell whether your

Introduction

parrot is a male or female. This is important especially if you plan on breeding them.

When it comes to the personality and behavior, poicephalus birds in general are reserved, shy but still easy going especially if you are their owner. They can easily adapt to their surroundings, and are also quite playful which is why you need to provide them with lots of stimuli.

Poicephalus birds react quite strongly to change compared to other parrot species which is why it's best to take it gradual if ever you need to implement any change (e.g. enclosure, diet, routine, other pet species etc.). One main characteristic of Poicephalus parrot species is that they have the ability to 'talk' though their voice is not that clear, and they don't learn as much words compare to other types of parrots. However, poicephalus species can mimic sounds pretty well. Some keepers actually mistake the beeping sound of their parrot for a microwave.

Parrots in general are flock – oriented creatures which is why they do very well with other species. If you want to form a bond with your poicephalus parrot, you/ your family need to sort of be a part of their flock. There are also some

Introduction

parrots that are known to be one – person birds, since in the wild they are loyal to only one mate, it's quite natural for them to also choose just one person as a lifetime companion.

Poicephalus parrots are also quite timid and wary to strangers but if they become acclimated to the members of the family, they are among the most affectionate breed. They will tend to crave for attention but they're not demanding. The great trait of poicephalus parrots is that they're not the screaming type making them excellent birds for patient and calm keepers. They can also learn different tricks, and they can be left alone for much of the day as long as you provide them with an adequate space, food, and toys to keep them stimulated. However, they will still need a daily dose of interaction from their owners.

Every poicephalus parrot species has its own personality, some of them are more interactive than others, some of them are quite shy and reserved, the key therefore is to get to know them through working with them so that their unique personality will eventually emerge, and both of you will be comfortable with one another.

Introduction

The next few chapters will help you in getting to know your pet parrot better, and also guide you on becoming the best bird keeper.

Introduction

Chapter One: Poicephalus Parrots in General

Poicephalus parrots or Ruppell's Parrots are regarded as one of the most outstanding companion birds especially for newbie parrot keepers. The Senegal poicephalus and Meyer poicephalus parrots in particular are considered by many pet keepers as the best poicephalus species because they are fairly easy to care for – thanks to their great personality and low – maintenance costs. What makes them very likeable is that they do not scream or 'talk' too much

Chapter One: Poicephalus Parrots in General

compared to common parrot species; they are sociable yet mischievous, fun, and affectionate birds.

Needless to say, they have big personalities wrapped up in small packages making them perfect housemates and family pets - not to mention suitable for those living in apartments.

Biological Information

The Poicephalus consists of various sub - species that are small to medium in size. On average, these birds measure around 8 to 13 inches in length, and weighs around 100 to 300 grams depending on the sub – species. They live for about 20 to 40 years (and sometimes more). The sub – species of Poicephalus that are commonly kept as pets include the following:

- Senegal Poicephalus (Species senegalus)
- Meyer's Poicephalus (Species meyeri)
- Red – Bellied Poicephalus (Species rufiventris)
- Cape Parrot (Species robustus)

Chapter One: Poicephalus Parrots in General

The Poicephalus sub – species that are not as common to keep as pets are the Jardine's Poicephalus (Species gulielmi), Brown – headed Poicephalus (Species Cryptoxanthus), Ruppel's Poicephalus (Species rueppellii), Niam – Niam Poicephalus (Species crassus), and Yellow – fronted Poicephalus (Species flavifrons). These kinds of bird species are often found in the wild and are quite aggressive to be kept as pets.

Parrot species under the genus Poicephalus usually have stocky bodies, and short tails. They generally have the same behavior as lovebirds but perhaps not as quick moving. This is especially true with Cape parrots since they are quite larger than the average Poicephalus species making them move quite slowly. However, lots of keepers also like to take care of this particular species because of their trademark 'smile' which is due to the shape of their beaks.

The smaller species typically sport a more vibrant colored body and also irises, and since they are small, they are very much inclined to engage in playful activities with their owners/ other birds. When these birds are aroused,

Chapter One: Poicephalus Parrots in General

they usually present a very impressive eye pinning combined with high pitched sounds.

Diet of Poicephalus Species

Poicephalus birds are naturally arboreal creatures. In the wild, their diet consists of nuts, fruits, and sometimes edible leaves. Even if they live together with their relatives, and congregate during eating time, sometimes they can still be quite aggressive to protect their food, and nesting/personal space. We will discuss more the kinds of food they eat, and how you can properly feed them in the next few chapters.

Potential Behavioral Problems

Poicephalus birds that have already established his/her own personal space or territory can be aggressive towards other birds. The confidence that makes these compact birds quite endearing can be shown through its bravery when it comes to defending its territory especially for mother birds that just gave birth; they will fight and defend their nesting space once they've established it. They do it through fluffing up their feathers to make them appear big, they'll pin their eyes, or they'll climb in its cage if an undesired trespasser enters their 'space.' Persistent invasion of their space either by you or other bird species can make your pet quite aggressive, and can also lead to biting you.

The good news is that aggressive behavior can be prevented, and also addressed. One way of avoiding aggressive behavior is by not forcing your bird to mate, and through slowly introducing it to another bird species if ever you decide to keep another one inside the same cage.

Items that you put inside the cage shouldn't be perceived as nest boxes, and their diet should be something that has more protein content and less fat. Such changes can help in controlling hormone levels that's related to reproduction. If you manage to control their hormone levels, your pet parrot will not trigger aggressive behaviors.

In addition to this, you can also alter the way you interact with your bird, and train it at a young age so that you can form a bond with him/her, and he/she can freely decide on what to do inside the cage without you always handling them. This will also help your bird to focus on more beneficial activities rather than in aggressive behaviors because they'll be stimulated, they will feel confident and also quite independent.

Behavioral Changes in Relation to Sexual Maturity

When Poicephalus parrots have reached sexually maturity (typically around the age of 2 to 3 years old), they tend to become quite aggressive, and increasingly want to feel independent. This transition usually catches a lot of owners off guard, but you have to understand that it's a phase – much like when kids become teenagers. Some keepers end up returning their pet parrots to a shelter or back to the breeder for the reason that their once cute and cuddly parrot has turned 'vicious,' or suddenly became easily agitated. There are some Poicephalus owners who are used to keeping smaller and gentler bird species like cockatiels, making it much harder for them to adjust to the sudden aggressive behavior of Poicephalus birds, and due to this, they often regard these birds as vicious. This leaves lots of owners frustrated, and that's primarily because they don't have any knowledge that birds also go through behavioral changes. Needless to say, this is just a phase.

Keepers who aren't aware of why their birds are suddenly quite aggressive, and wanted to be left alone often result into them returning the aggression through shouting at the birds, depriving them of their needs, spraying them with water, hurting the bird, or deliberately punishing them. Doing all of these can just make the situation worse, and your Poicephalus parrot will be harder to tame, handle, or train. Your bird will either become too aggressive, or too scared of people. In addition to that, the relationship and bond that you've built with your pet will be damaged, and if you hit them, they can also suffer injuries that could result to death.

If you find your parrot becoming aggressive, you can handle it using various techniques to keep their aggressiveness at bay. However, you have to understand that even if you do that, your parrot will never be the same as it was before undergoing this behavioral change – and that's okay. Like teenagers, this is all part of 'growing up,'

Chapter One: Poicephalus Parrots in General

you can't really control it so the best way to handle this is to change your approach and be extra patient.

You'll need to change the way you interact with your juvenile Poicephalus to accommodate their new attitude or mindset while reinforcing your bond and trust with them at the same time. Keep in mind that your goal is to be your parrot's best friend, and allow him/her to thrive as an adult. You must change along with them and show them that you'll be there no matter what just as they are always there for you.

Distribution and Habitat in the Wild

The Poicephalus parrots are endemic to African countries particularly in the southern regions of Angola, and northern – central regions of Namibia.

In Namibia, these birds predominantly live in rivers like the Hoarusib River, and Swakop River in Namibia. They are also usually found in Acacia erioloba trees and Faidherbia albida trees while in Angola, they mostly occur in arid woodlands.

Chapter One: Poicephalus Parrots in General

In the wild, Poicephalus parrots are also distributed in various seed – bearing trees, and are sporadically spread over wider areas particularly in higher altitudes. These birds are also seen in vegetation zones.

These birds prefer to create their nests in holes of tall trees, usually in downward – facing hollows so that it will be difficult to access by potential predators.

When it comes to creating nests, Poicephalus birds tend to get competitive and territorial, and if they don't find an adequate nesting place in the wild, this prevents them from breeding. According to researchers, Poicephalus parrot mother lays their eggs around January to March, and their babies leave the nests around April to June; a clutch typically contains just 3 to 5 eggs.

These birds also feed on various flowers and fruits, nectars, shoots, and even insects. Their diet in the wild constantly shifts throughout the year as one tree comes into fruition followed by others.

Chapter One: Poicephalus Parrots in General

Threats and Conservation Status

The illegal trade in the wild is the biggest threat to most parrots and bird species in general. In Namibia, illegal trade of this species are quite rampant because investigations found out that around 600 to 1,000 birds are exported illegally to South African countries and also in Europe particularly in Germany. Around 80% of these wild – caught birds die during transit, while others tend to suffer illnesses. These species are usually caught by farm laborers where they use bird traps to capture 3 to 6 birds at a time. They then smuggle it across the border to South Africa.

Even if it's illegal to capture and trade these wild species, lots of people are still doing it because wild – caught birds are usually profitable especially if it comes in pairs. Over – exploitation in commercial farmlands where the Poicephalus species often occurs is quite high but thanks to the European Union, bird exports are now completely ban creating a decline in illegal trading though some are still doing this practice.

The best way to help the environment and to stop the continuation of these illegal activities is to ensure that you

Chapter One: Poicephalus Parrots in General

only buy from legal breeders and bird hobbyists. Try not to buy from pet stores because sometimes the owners get their supply from illegal pet traders but they're not aware that the birds are smuggled.

When it comes to the conservation status, as of now, the populations of these birds are stabled due to the decline of illegal trading unlike before where it is classified as 'near – threatened.' It's not globally classified as threatened but because of the previous over – exploitation cases, these parrots are under the Specially Protected species especially in Namibia. The Poicephalus parrots are under the Appendix II of the CITES (Convention on International Trade and Endangered Species of Wild Fauna and Flora).

Chapter One: Poicephalus Parrots in General

Chapter Two: Poicephalus Species and Sub - Species

This chapter will cover the family of the Poicephalus birds. It'll be best for you to know the other species and sub – species under this family so that you'd also be aware of their unique characteristics and their differences in their physical attributes. This will help you determine which species will suit best for you/ your family, and you'll also get to know a bit of their background especially on how they live in the wild. The various species of Poicephalus parrots covered here are just the most common species in captivity, and in the wild.

Chapter Two: Poicephalus Species and Sub - Species
Abyssinian Parrots

- Commonly known as Red – bellied Parrots or Red – breasted Parrots

- These species are quite larger than the Senegal Poicephalus but almost similar in stature and body type. The average size of the Red – Bellied parrot is 8.5 to 8.8 inches in length or around 22 cm.

- The wings, heads, and backs are greyish – brown in color while the lower back area are yellowish – green in color with blue tinge. The breasts and cheeks are splashed with orange while the underwing coverts and thighs are blue – green in color.

- These species are distributed in East Africa particularly in the southern regions of Pangani district which is near Tanzania, and also in Central Ethiopia.

Chapter Two: Poicephalus Species and Sub - Species

Angola Brown Parrots

- Has quite a similar appeal as Meyer's Parrots but has a grey – brown colored head but with a much darker shade in its upper breast. They are larger than the size of a Meyer's species, and also lack a yellow color in its crown.

- These species are found in the northern and central regions of Angola, and also in various areas in Congo.

Brown - headed Parrots

- The Brown – headed parrots are mostly green in color, and it sports a brownish – grey color in its head and nape (neck). Their wings and thighs also have a yellow shade.

- These species are found in the southern area of Mozambique, and the eastern regions of South Africa.

Chapter Two: Poicephalus Species and Sub - Species

Cape Parrots

- Cape parrots are also known as Tori Parrots or Brown – necked parrots.

- The head sports a brownish – green to a brownish – yellow color with dark brown spots and sometimes dull green streak.

- These species are distributed in Western and Eastern Africa, South Africa, and also the Eastern Cape regions.

Damaraland Brown Parrots

- Also looks a lot like Meyer's parrot but sports a brownish – grey head, lacks a yellow color in its crown, and has a darkish grey shade in its upper chest area.

- Damaraland Brown Parrots are often found in Central regions of Namibia, Southern areas Angola, and north – west side of Botswana.

Chapter Two: Poicephalus Species and Sub - Species

East African Brown Parrots

- Another Poicephalus species that looks like the Meyer's Parrot is the East – African Brown Parrot. This bird species sports a brownish – grey head with its upper chest area slightly has a darker shade. Its crown has some yellow feathers in it.

- These species are distributed in northern regions of Zambia, and Malawi, Southeast regions of Congo and Kenya as well as Tanzania.

Kuhl's Cape Parrots

- This Poicephalus species sports a grey or brown neck, has orange splashed in the shoulders, has a darkish green chest area, and a slightly lighter shade of green in its thighs and lower area.

- It's mostly found in South Africa.

Chapter Two: Poicephalus Species and Sub - Species

Jardine's Parrot

- Jardine's Parrot is one of the most common Poicephalus parrot species that are kept as pets. They are also known as red – headed parrots.

- These birds sport an orange – red color on its forehead up to its crown including its wings and thigh area.

- They are typically distributed around the Congo River

Masai Red - headed Parrots

- The Masai Red – headed parrot species looks somewhat the same with Jardine's Parrot but the orange – red color found in its forehead is not extended up to its crown but rather just above the beak.

- These birds are found in the southern regions of Kenya, and northern areas of Tanzania usually in the highlands.

Chapter Two: Poicephalus Species and Sub - Species

Meyer's Parrots

- The Meyer's Poicephalus species is also one of the most common parrots kept as pets. It sports a greyish – brown plumage. It also has yellow spots on its thighs and wings.

- These species are distributed in the western regions of Ethiopia, and South Chad but became quite popular in America around the 1960's.

- It inhabits wooded grasslands and scrubs in the wild.

- Unlike Senegal parrots, Meyer's parrots take time in adjusting to a new environment, and these birds tend to be shyer than their relatives but once you've gained their trust they are a loving companion.

- Meyer's parrots don't do well in small cages so make sure that you acquire a suitable enclosure for their size.

Chapter Two: Poicephalus Species and Sub - Species

Niam - Niam Parrots

- Niam – niam parrots sports a brownish – grey oor yellow – olive colored head and nape. Their body color is mostly green.

- Niam – niam birds are distributed in Chad, the Eastern regions of Cameroon, in southwest regions of Sudan, in Central Africa, and in Congo.

Orange - bellied Parrots

- Orange – bellied parrots have some similarities with the Senegal parrot but it's just slightly paler.

- It sports a grey – colored head, and has deep orange coloration in the abdominal area.

- These birds are found in the northern region of Cameroon, south – western regions of Chad, and Eastern side and north – eastern regions of Nigeria.

Chapter Two: Poicephalus Species and Sub - Species

Orange - crowned Parrots

- The Orange – crowned species are also quite similar looking as Jardine's parrot but the main differences include an orange forecrown, and a reddish – orange splash of colors in its wings.

- It is also slightly smaller in size than Jardine's parrot species.

- These birds are found in the southern areas of Ghana, and in Liberia.

Orange - faced Parrots

- Has quite a similar look with the Yellow – faced parrot except that the face has a vibrant shade of orange color.

- These birds are found in the Gila River, in Masango area, and also in the south – western regions of Ethiopia.

Red - Vented Parrots

- It sports a grey – colored head with dark green upperparts, and has a red or sometimes orange –

Chapter Two: Poicephalus Species and Sub - Species

colored abdomen. It's also quite similar looking as the Senegal parrot.

- These birds are found in Ghana, the eastern and western areas of Nigeria, and also in Ivory Coast.

Reichenow's Orange - bellied Parrots

- Has a slightly paler shade than the Senegal parrot, and it also sports a grey – colored head. Its abdominal area has a deep orange shade.

- These birds are found in the northern areas of Cameroon, in the eastern regions of Nigeria, and in South – western areas of Chad.

Rüppell's Parrots, Ruppel's or Rueppel's Parrots

- Sports a darkish grey head, has yellow spots on their wings, and upper legs, and its plumage has a darkish brown color. This bird also has a friendly demeanor just like its relatives.

Chapter Two: Poicephalus Species and Sub - Species

- These birds are found in the Southwest areas of Luanda, and Angola as well as in Central regions of Namibia.

- Another popular Poicephalus species inhabits open woodlands, and plains.

Senegal Parrots

- Has a grey – colored head, has a green colored chest area with yellow - colored abdomen. These birds have powerful beaks, a bit timid but very friendly birds.

- These birds are found in the Western Africa particularly in Mali, Mauritania, Senegal, Guinea, Guinea – Bissau, Gambia, and Lobos Island. It's also distributed in Chad, Nigeria, and Cameroon.

- Senegal parrots are the most popular sub – species of the Poicephalus family. It inhabits Savannahs, forests, and also farms.

- They mostly eat insects, rice, and corn in the wild.

Chapter Two: Poicephalus Species and Sub - Species

Somalia Red - bellied Parrots

- Has quite a similar look like the Red – Bellied parrot species but only sports a brownish – grey head, and the chest area are slightly paler.

- These birds are found in the Somalia, and eastern regions of Ethiopia.

South African Brown Parrots

- Sports yellow markings in the head, and a green – colored abdomen. It has a quite similar look as the Meyer's parrot.

- These birds are found in the South Africa, Zimbabwe and Botswana.

Tanzanian Brown - headed Parrots

- Has quite a similar look as the Brown – headed parrot but sports a more brownish – olive colored head with yellow – green colored belly, chest, and undertail coverts.

Chapter Two: Poicephalus Species and Sub - Species

- These birds are found in the Save River of Mozambique, eastern regions of Tanzania, southern side of Mali, and south – east of Kenya.

Uganda Yellow - shouldered Parrots

- Also known as Kenya Meyer Parrot, it sports yellow markings on its head and has a green – colored abdomen.

- These birds are found in Uganda, and western Kenya and Tanzania.

Yellow - faced Parrots

- The Yellow – Faced parrot sports a yellow cheeks, crown, and forehead with a green – colored body.

- These birds are found in central and northern areas of Ethiopia.

Zanzibar Brown - headed Parrots

- This is a disputed sub – species of the Poicephalus family.

Chapter Two: Poicephalus Species and Sub - Species

- Has a similar look as the Brown – headed parrot but only slightly larger and has an olive – brown colored head.

- These birds are found in the Pemba Islands and Zanzibar

Chapter Three: Acquiring, Feeding and Housing Poicephalus Parrots

This chapter will guide you on where you can get a Poicephalus parrot, what to feed them, and how you can house them properly. When it comes to acquiring a pet parrot, we will discuss the benefits of getting one from a hobbyist, or adopting from a rescue center (if ever a Poicephalus species is available) because many first – time keepers make the mistake of buying one from cheap backyard breeders or from pet stores. When it comes to feeding, we'll take a closer look at the commercially

Chapter Three: Acquiring, Feeding & Housing Poicephalus Parrots

available brands out there that you might want for your new pet. You'll also learn the housing essentials for your parrot.

Benefits of Acquiring Poicephalus Parrots from Hobbyists

- The major advantage of purchasing a Poicephalus parrot from a hobbyist or a reputable breeder is that you're sure that your pet is well – taken care of from breeding to birth. Avian hobbyists are considered 'experts,' and even if they do not have any formal distinction like an avian vet has, they're still a great source of healthy and quality birds.

- It's best that you get your bird from a reputable breeder instead of buying from pet stores because usually most animals acquired from pet stores are bought from breeders that do mass breeding, and sometimes most pet store owners aren't aware that

Chapter Three: Acquiring, Feeding & Housing Poicephalus Parrots

some birds are illegally caught in the wild. One of the major benefits is that you'll be assured that the birds aren't illegally acquired from smugglers. Legit breeders do this not just to make money but also out of passion.

- There are many avian hobbyists that breed birds, and some of them are experts in particular bird species; what you want to do is to search for an avian hobbyist that's also an expert in Poicephalus parrots. However, if you can't seem to find that, acquiring one from a parrot expert will do.

- Getting your pet Poicephalus from a legit and homegrown hobbyist will also enable you to get a 'mentor' that you can seek advice from since they're the ones who raised these birds from birth until a young age. You'll get to have a sort of an 'after – sale' service because hobbyists do care for their pets.

Chapter Three: Acquiring, Feeding & Housing Poicephalus Parrots

Benefits of Adopting from Rescue Centers

- I guess one of the main benefits of acquiring a pet parrot from a rescue center is that you're literally going to save a life. Most birds or animals in rescue centers are usually from owners who have already abandoned these poor creatures for various reasons – usually because they've lost interest in it, or they can't properly take care of it. By rescuing a pet, you'll be doing something good for the environment and for the bird itself since it will get to have a new home and probably a well – deserved keeper.

- Rescue centers sometimes do a personality test so that they can match you up with a bird that's quite complementary of your own characteristics. You can pre - determine which bird species is best for you through this personality test. After having gone through all the steps and the training or other activities that the rescue centers have you do, you can

Chapter Three: Acquiring, Feeding & Housing Poicephalus Parrots

now have the opportunity to foster or adopt through them.

- When you adopt a lovebird, it's usually at a much lesser cost in your part. The cost of buying a bird from a reputable private breeder versus acquiring one through adoption is very significant.

- Rescue centers are much easier to search for because most of them are legit. Your avian vet can give you lists of local avian rescue centers.

- Rescue centers also give out different resources that are going to be beneficial for you as a new bird owner.

- Adopting a Poicephalus parrot from rescue centers may be quite hard since you don't really have any other option unlike if you acquire from a parrot breeder but it's still worth a try than you buying from a pet store because the last thing you want to do is

Chapter Three: Acquiring, Feeding & Housing Poicephalus Parrots

contribute to the ongoing phenomenon where parrots are being exploited, and illegally traded in the wild.

Searching for an Avian Veterinarian

- Finding a good local vet by visiting AAV.org (Association of Avian Veterinarian), it's a wonderful resource because you can easily go to their website, and easily search the vet of your choice.

- The website will provide you with a list of licensed avian vets in your area of residence. It'll surely save you the time and effort in finding a reputable one.

- After choosing your avian vet, you can then call them up so that you can further interview them, and see if they are real experts in parrots particularly in the Poicephalus breed. You can ask questions related to the parrot breed, and this is also the time to ask them how much their consultation fee is so that you can

Chapter Three: Acquiring, Feeding & Housing Poicephalus Parrots

also compare their rates to your other prospective vets.

- Another great way is using social media or getting a recommendation from a friend (either through parrot forums, blogs, social media websites, or through a personal referral).

Micro – chipping Your Poicephalus

When it comes to keeping your Poicephalus parrot safe, it's important that your pet has a leg band. Leg bands functions as your bird's identification card. It usually contains the information about the bird, when the bird has hatched, and other important information from the breeder of your pet like the state where your breeder is doing his business etc. It's up to you if you want to remove your parrot's leg band; some people don't like to have leg band on their bird's feet while some don't mind. If ever your bird is fidgeting with its leg band, you can have your avian vet remove it for you.

Chapter Three: Acquiring, Feeding & Housing Poicephalus Parrots

If you want your Poicephalus parrot to be permanently identified, you can choose to have a microchip implanted on its skin. Micro - chipping in birds is pretty much the same procedure that is used in other household pets like dogs and cats. This is the process where vets surgically implant a chip under the animal's skin. The chip contains the owner's information or the bird species information so that they can be identified if ever they get lost.

Leg bands and micro - chipping are the legally recognized form of identification for parrots, and other household animals in general. It's particularly helpful if you are always travelling with your pet or you like to take them outside the house since it will lessen the risk of them totally getting lost in case they flew away from you.

If you want to know how the identification will be implanted in your parrot, it's best to consult your avian vet so that he/she can further explain to you the benefits of doing so as well as the process and also how much it would cost for the procedure.

Chapter Three: Acquiring, Feeding & Housing Poicephalus Parrots

Cage Essentials and House Set - Up

Parrot Cage

- A parrot cage is where your pet Poicephalus will spend most of their time. Depending on the size, quality, durability, and the materials or cage accessories included, cages usually cost around between $40 and $150 and up. A standard bird cage mostly comes with a perch and stainless steel bowls. Make sure that there is enough space for your pet, and consider their current size (this can vary among Poicephalus species).

- Make sure to get something that measures 2 x 2 x 2 foot cubes. Poicephalus parrots are territorial animals, and they are also arboreal. They need a space where they can flap their wings. Change the size as they get larger, and adjust accordingly.

Chapter Three: Acquiring, Feeding & Housing Poicephalus Parrots

- Don't buy a round or vertical cage because if you do, your Poicephalus parrot might only utilize the highest horizontal space of the cage – this will restrict them if you bought a tall but narrow cage or a round one. The reason why birds don't prefer round cages is because it doesn't give them that sense of protection.

- It's highly recommended that you buy longer cages with the minimum measure aforementioned so that they can use the entire length of the cage to go back and forth, and maximize the space of the enclosure.

- Parrots like the Poicephalus species usually like to spend their time in a corner where they feel safe. In the wild, most of them like to hide inside tight spaces and create nests in narrow hollows of trees because it offers a sense of privacy and safety for them which round cages don't offer.

- For the bar spacing of the cage, it should at least have a ½ to 1 inch bar spacing so that your parrot wouldn't

Chapter Three: Acquiring, Feeding & Housing Poicephalus Parrots

be able to squeeze itself into the bars and sneak out. Some cage have bar spaces that are quite wide so ensure that it is appropriately spaced for the size of your Poicephalus parrot.

- You might also need to buy clips that could secure the doors to prevent your bird from escaping because some Poicephalus parrot are really smart and curious and they'll try to open their door cages.

- Ensure that you purchase a stainless type of parrot cage so that your pet wouldn't ingest any paint that can be toxic for them.

- The bird cage that you'll purchase may also come with a bird protector. The purpose of that is to protect your pet from mites but you can also choose to remove it because it's usually not that effective. Make sure to cover part of the cage so that it will act as their safe zone where they can hide.

Chapter Three: Acquiring, Feeding & Housing Poicephalus Parrots

Cage Accessories

- You'll need to purchase two to three stainless steel bowls. You don't want to buy a plastic bowl because it holds molds, and bacteria that will be harmful for your pet. It's also easier to clean, easy to slip inside your parrot's cage, and most importantly, it doesn't harbor molds and bacteria or leave any food smells unlike plastic bowls. Make sure to clean these bowls everyday with lukewarm water. It's better if you have more than two ceramic or stainless bowls so that you have an alternative. Some bird cages already comes with a bowl feeder that's attached to the little doors so just make sure to thoroughly wash it.

- You can buy separate food bowls in online stores like Amazon for around $5 and up depending on the size.

- Another important cage accessory is perches; you can get two to three perches for your Poicephalus

Chapter Three: Acquiring, Feeding & Housing Poicephalus Parrots

parrot/s. Perches will cost anywhere between $10 and up depending on what type you buy. You want to make sure that the perch is sturdy enough. Make sure that you replace the perches after being used for a few weeks so that the nails of your pet don't get filed.

- When it comes to toys, you must provide a variety, and something that's mentally stimulating since Poicephalus parrots are curious creatures. Only keep around six things inside the cage. You can rotate toys but make sure not to put them all at once.

- Another cage accessory is bedding or at least a sheet underneath the cage. Beddings like a newspaper or paper towels will keep everything clean. The material is also recyclable, and easy to replace.

- Regular baths for your pet parrot is part of good hygiene which is why you need to invest in a misting system or a spray bottle. This is a good way for you to ensure that their skin and feathers stay healthy.

Chapter Three: Acquiring, Feeding & Housing Poicephalus Parrots

Misting the cage is also a way for your pet bird to get hydrated.

Other Parrot Essentials

Cage Cleaners

- You need to buy wipes, paper towels, soap, cleaning detergent, and wash cloths. Paper towels are a major necessity when keeping any kinds of birds; you'll use it for wiping, cleaning after your bird, and drying stuff up. Cage cleaners may cost you a total of $100 or more.

Food and Treats

- Your Poicephalus parrot's primary diet is a commercial pellet that's usually a fruit blend feeds. In addition to this, you'll also need to provide your pet with a variety of fruit and veggies.

Chapter Three: Acquiring, Feeding & Housing Poicephalus Parrots

- Poicephalus parrots and parrot birds in general love seeds and treats! You want to get seeds that will promote an active healthy diet for captive birds. You can give your parrot a few seed treats a day. Such treats may cost you around $10 to $15 per bag but can last for around 3 months.

Travel Cage

- A carrier cage or a travel cage will cost you around $90 and up depending on the size and brand. A travel carrier cage is important if you love to go road tripping with your family, or if you need to simply get your Poicephalus parrot to the vet as it will need to be transferred safely.

- Just like a normal cage, you'll need to provide a few things inside the travel cage to keep your pet Poicephalus occupied. You're also going to need a new perch which will cost anywhere between $8 and $10.

Chapter Three: Acquiring, Feeding & Housing Poicephalus Parrots

- When you see the perch starting to fray, you need to replace it. Don't buy a plastic perch because it'll be slippery for your Poicephalus parrot, and will most likely cause injuries. You may need to also put a few treats and at least 1 or 2 toys to keep boredom at bay.

Housebreaking Your Poicephalus Parrot

Here are the steps on what you need to do to get your new pet parrot transition easily and comfortably to its new home and environment.

Step #1: Transfer your bird from the travel cage to its actual bird cage. You need to get the parrot out of the travel cage, and you can do that by bringing the travel cage near the opening of its actual enclosure.

Step #2: Make sure to balance the box on the edge of the cage door. You need to make sure that the door (of your travel cage) wouldn't slide around otherwise you wouldn't be able to control it. This is why it's important to get an

Chapter Three: Acquiring, Feeding & Housing Poicephalus Parrots

appropriate cage size because it will be much more difficult for you in trying to get your parrot out of the box if the cage is too big or too small.

Step #3: Lure your Poicephalus parrot with a bowl filled with treats until the bird eventually reaches the door of actual cage. You need to slowly open the door (of the actual cage), and then offer your bird with some treats to entice him/her to crossover to the other side. Once you've successfully done that, close the door, walk away, and leave your pet alone so that he/she can adjust to the new environment.

Step #4: Give your pet some space but don't isolate him/her. This is especially true if you bought your Poicephalus parrot from the pet store. Give time to adjust in their new house but don't just leave your parrot in a separate room or in an isolated area because the parrot may not be used to isolation since it is exposed in constant stimulation and interaction from people viewing them in pet stores. If you happen to buy a parrot from a pet store, make

Chapter Three: Acquiring, Feeding & Housing Poicephalus Parrots

sure to place its cage in a location where there's foot traffic or interaction from you/your family.

Step #5: Earn the trust of your newfound Poicephalus parrot. You can start gaining your pet's trust by always offering fresh food and water every single day. Do this for at least the first few days coupled with daily morning greetings, and you calling them by their names.

Step #6: Entice them with food and treats. This is one great way of earning the trust and winning your pet's affection. You need to make sure that they are well – fed. Throw the old food from yesterday, and replace it with fresh food using a newly washed stainless bowl or another brand new bowl. The reason why you need to offer the food in an appropriate bowl is that it will create noise that will make your Poicephalus parrot excited to eat. Make sure to take note of what kind of treats your bird prefers so that you know what to feed them.

Chapter Three: Acquiring, Feeding & Housing Poicephalus Parrots

Step #7: Always interact with them. I'm not saying you constantly bother your bird in its cage. What you can do is to talk to him/her calmly while feeding them on the side of the cage. What you need to do is to just slide the food bowl inside the cage. Do not open the door, do not stick your hand out inside the cage or hand fed your bird, do not handle your bird in its first few weeks. This is very important, regardless of your bird's age, type or where it was acquire or how it was raised.

Step #8: Do not handle your parrot in the first few days to a week. Parrots are naturally fearful creatures especially if they haven't adjusted yet to their new environment which is why you need to earn their trust and be patient with them. Once you've built your trust to your parrot overtime, it will assume that you are part of their flock. If your pet bird already treat you as one of their 'family,' it will eventually be much easier to bond with him/her. Make sure to always leave a treat behind every time you go out and say goodbye to them so that he/she knows that you care.

Chapter Three: Acquiring, Feeding & Housing Poicephalus Parrots

Step #9: Lights off! It's important to ensure that all the lights are off in the room when night comes otherwise it will keep your pet bird awake. You can cover half of the bird cage with a towel every night, and just uncover it every morning to simulate day and night.

Step #10: Let them be. Leave your pet Poicephalus 'alone' for the first seven days. Provide them with food and water as well as toys and perches to keep boredom at bay. Always interact with them and just let them know you're there. After about a week or so, you can try to handle your bird but don't rush this process. It will come naturally once you've already formed a bond with them.

Feeding Your Poicephalus Parrots

Knowing what to feed your Poicephalus parrot is essential because the right diet will keep them healthy and active. Owners usually offer a various mix of commercial pellets but it's also important that the brand you'll buy

Chapter Three: Acquiring, Feeding & Housing Poicephalus Parrots

doesn't use any fillers or artificial coloring because such ingredients wouldn't provide good nutrition. In addition to commercial pellets, you can also feed your parrot with whole grains, mullets, and oats although these things are already included in commercial bird foods.

Parrots like other animals are also prone to illnesses like obesity. Obesity is the result of an improper nutrition, if you are feeding your bird ingredients that are high in fats, he/she will definitely get obese over the long term. The goal is to make your pet lean, active, and healthy – all of these things can be achieved with the right diet.

The right bird diet should contain 20% grains, around 5% to 10% seeds, and 40% commercial pellet. In addition to that, you should also include fruits and vegetables in your parrot's diet. Try offering the following:

- Cucumbers
- Artichokes
- Baby greens
- Broccolis
- Small sprouts

Chapter Three: Acquiring, Feeding & Housing Poicephalus Parrots

- Apples
- Tropical fruits

For an average size Poicephalus parrot, you need to feed around 1 to 1 ½ tablespoons of commercial pellets every day. This amount will vary depending on the kind of pellet you offer, and also the size or age of your Poicephalus pet. It's highly recommended that you consult your avian vet so that you'll know exactly how much to feed your bird, how often, and the kind of diet suitable for him/her.

Here are other things to keep in mind when feeding your pet:

- Most parrots including Poicephalus species love to feed on vegies and fruits but you have to keep in mind that changing their diet should be done in a gradual manner.

- It's also important to note that what's safe for people may not always be safe for birds. Never you're your

Chapter Three: Acquiring, Feeding & Housing Poicephalus Parrots

pet with avocados, chocolates, caffeine, and other toxic matters.

❖ Parrots are omnivores, you can feed them commercial pellets, grains, nutria fruit blends, fresh fruit slices and veggies, and of course fresh and clean water.

❖ When picking a commercial food, make sure that the brand contains natural ingredients, and doesn't use any sort of fillers.

❖ If you plan on keeping more than one Poicephalus parrot you must provide multiple feeding and drinking stations so that they won't fight over the food you offer them.

❖ When thinking about what to feed your pet parrot, always keep in mind how they do it in the wild so that you can understand their preferences.

Chapter Three: Acquiring, Feeding & Housing Poicephalus Parrots

- ❖ Sometimes, your parrot won't be able to eat all the pellets or grains that put in their bowl so make sure that you throw away all the uneaten foods and always put fresh ones because if you don't, the uneaten foods will harbor bacteria and molds which can be harmful for your bird's health as it can become contaminated.

- ❖ To avoid uneaten meals, just initially put a small amount and maybe add a little more if need be. This way you can also save on your bird's food consumption.

- ❖ Make sure to monitor your parrot whenever they are eating. This is one way of knowing if your pet prefers the diet you are giving him/her, and it will let you know if your bird is ill; sudden loss of appetite may indicate that your pet is sick. If you notice that your pet doesn't normally eat as it should, it's wise to bring him/her to an avian vet as soon as possible for a check – up.

Chapter Three: Acquiring, Feeding & Housing Poicephalus Parrots

Recommended Food Brands

This section will cover the top 10 most recommended food brands or bird diet suitable for your Poicephalus parrot. You'll be provided with the overview of the product, the ingredients it contains, and the feeding amount for each. This will help you determine which one is best for your bird's diet.

#1: Oven Fresh Bites Natural Baked Diet

Vets and avian nutritionists highly recommend Oven Fresh Bites because it's a diet filled with vitamins, minerals, and protein that your Poicephalus parrot will require to achieve a great health and long life. Each nugget is finely baked, and it offers not just whole grains but also various organic ingredients such as oatmeal, cranberries, sunflower seeds, apples, banana, blueberries, red bell peppers, peas, and carrots. There are no added artificial colors or sugar making it one of the best formulated diets for parrots in the

Chapter Three: Acquiring, Feeding & Housing Poicephalus Parrots

market today. It comes in a re - sealable bag to keep the ingredients fresh.

The Oven Fresh Bites Natural Baked Diet is a meal intended for medium to large parrot species like Senegal Poicephalus parrot, African Greys, Macaws, Conures, Cockatoos, Caiques, and Amazon parrots.

When it comes to purchasing commercial formulated diet, it's also important that you take note of the ingredients that come with it, and avoid fillers or unnecessary food content. Here are some of the other important ingredients of this formulated diet:

- Sunflower Chips
- Mixed Feed Nuts
- Freeze Dried Papaya
- Banana Chips
- Soybean Meal
- Alfalfa Meal
- Polyphosphate (source of Vitamin C)
- Vitamin E Supplement
- Vitamin B12 Supplement

Chapter Three: Acquiring, Feeding & Housing Poicephalus Parrots

- Vitamin D3 Supplement
- Vitamin A Acetate
- Riboflavin Supplement
- Folic Acid
- Thiamine Mononitrate

#2: Lafeber's Garden Veggie Parrot Nutri-Berries

The Garden Veggie Parrot Nutri – Berries by Lafeber is a formulated mixed diet consisting of healthy ingredients such as savory peanuts, cracked corn, and hulled canary seed. This is a fun meal for your pet Poicephalus because this food will enable your bird to thrive on foraging stimulation and also provides beak exercise. Feeding your bird with this formulated mix is a great way to get him/her into veggies.

When it comes to feeding amounts, here's how you can introduce Lafeber's Garden Veggie Parrot Nutri – Berries diet on your Poicephalus' current diet:

Chapter Three: Acquiring, Feeding & Housing Poicephalus Parrots

- You can combine this food mix with whatever diet your bird is currently in. Once you see your parrot eating the Nutri – berries, you can gradually discontinue the previous formulated diet or seed mix.

- Most parrots easily accept the Nutri – berries diet right away but if ever your pet doesn't initially eat the mix, what you can do is to flatten out the Nutri – berries, and mix it with the current pellet mix until this new diet is accepted.

- When your Poicephalus parrot already accepted this new change of diet, you can feed him/her as needed in a 12 – hour period.

- Make sure that your bird first eats all what you've placed in its food bowl before adding more if need be.

- Ideally, your Poicephalus parrot should be fed twice a day but consult your vet for exact amount as it will depend on its current size and age.

Chapter Three: Acquiring, Feeding & Housing Poicephalus Parrots

Lafeber's Garden Veggie Parrot Nutri – Berries contains around 10% of Crude Protein, 6% Crude Fat, 5% Crude Fiber, 0.31% of Omega – 3 Fatty Acids, 3.91% of Omega – 6 Fatty Acids, and 14% Moisture. Here are some of the other important ingredients of this formulated diet:

- Oat grouts
- Red millet
- Safflower
- Soybean meal
- Peanut granules
- Wheat
- Carrots
- Whole egg
- Broccoli
- Vitamin E supplement
- Ascorbic acid
- Niacin supplement
- Vitamin B12 supplement
- Vitamin D3 supplement
- Folic acid

Chapter Three: Acquiring, Feeding & Housing Poicephalus Parrots

- Copper lysine complex

#3: Roudybush California Blend Adult Bird Maintenance Food

RoudyBush is another favorite brand of most birds. We highly recommend the California Blend Adult Bird Maintenance diet for your growing Poicephalus parrot. This delectable diet will definitely entice your pet bird to have an appetite. It's made of fresh veggies and fruits. It's a no – waste diet mix that contains pieces from wholesome fruits like plums, dried peaches, tomatoes, bell peppers, apricots, cabbage, and carrots combined with the signature Roudybush's daily maintenance pellets.

This steam – pelleted diet mix also retain many beneficial nutriets, eliminates harmful bacteria in your parrot, minimizes waste, and an easy – to – feed parrot mix that's fortified with vitamins and minerals. You won't need to add other vitamin/ mineral supplements, artificial colors and sugars because it's already included in this pelleted diet.

Chapter Three: Acquiring, Feeding & Housing Poicephalus Parrots

This formulated pellet diet is also suitable for various parrot species including Poicephalus birds.

To ensure that you are feeding your Poicephalus parrot the right amount of pellet size, take note of the feeding instructions below:

- Feed the Roudybush California Blend Adult Bird Maintenance mix as a sole diet. Don't provide other vitamin or mineral add – ons. You can feed your bird with healthy treats as an additional food but give it in moderate amounts.

- You must also ensure that you monitor your parrot's diet by evaluating his/her droppings.

- If your Poicephalus parrot hasn't eaten pellets yet, they may not recognize it as food first but be patient as it will take time to switch them to eating a pelleted mix. Pellets are usually lower in fats compared to a seed mix. Some parrots and bird species accept crumbles or a pellet mix diet when they realize that it

Chapter Three: Acquiring, Feeding & Housing Poicephalus Parrots

is edible while some birds take time to try this new type of diet.

- If ever your parrots are a finicky one, and you want to switch him/her into this type of diet, what you need to do is to completely remove the current diet, and fill its food bowls with this pelleted mix. It's also ideal to weigh your bird first thing in the morning on the day of the diet switch, weigh your bird every morning thereafter.

- If in case your parrot loses 3 to 5% of its body weight after you offer the new pelleted mix, put it back on its old diet for about 1 to 2 weeks before switching again, following the same weight monitoring as aforementioned.

- If in case you weren't able to weigh your pet, what you can do is to change the beddings or newspapers at the bottom of the cage on the day of the switch so that you can monitor your pet's droppings. If the

Chapter Three: Acquiring, Feeding & Housing Poicephalus Parrots

feces is small, and is either black or dark green in color, it could mean that your bird is not eating the pellet mix. What you can do is to continue offering the food for 2 full days (for smaller Poicephalus species), and 3 full days (for larger Poicephalus species) before making a conclusion. Once you see that your pet's droppings is still anorexic (black/ dark green in color), you may put the parrot back to its old diet for about 1 to 2 weeks before trying to switch it again. Some finicky birds take about 3 attempts before adapting the new diet so be patient and just monitor them if you want them to take this kind of pelleted mix.

What you can also do is to act as if you're eating the Roudybush diet because sometimes birds will try it out for themselves if they see their keepers eating it (they value you since you're part of the 'flock'). Most parrots like Roudybush pellets once they've already tasted it making it quite an easy convertion but still make sure to monitor their poop or

Chapter Three: Acquiring, Feeding & Housing Poicephalus Parrots

weigh them out so you can see if they can completely switch to this new pelleted diet.

Here are some of the other important ingredients of this formulated diet:

- Ground Corn
- Dried Carrots
- Ground Wheat
- Dried Bell Peppers
- Dried Peaches
- Soybean Oil
- Dried Cabbage
- Dried Plums
- Dried Tomatoes
- Dried Apricots
- Alfalfa
- Tartaric Acid
- Natural Apple Flavoring
- Vitamin A Acetate
- Zinc Oxide
- Vitamin D3 Supplement

Chapter Three: Acquiring, Feeding & Housing Poicephalus Parrots

#4: Harrison's High Potency Fine Bird Food

Another pellet mix that vets also recommend is the High Potency Fine Bird Food by Harrison's. It's made out of premium and certified organic ingredients that's mostly targeted for parrots/ birds requiring critical nutrition in times of illness and/ or transitions. It's a vet – formulated pellet mix that is required by avian vets whenever a bird is recovering from an illness, breeding, molting, weaning, or if you are going to switch him/ her from a seed – only diet. This parrot mix is perfect not just for Poicephalus species but also for lories, cockatiels, lovebirds, conures, and other small to medium parrot species. No supplementation is also required and it comes in a re – sealable package.

The High Potency Formula is mainly for the following conditions:

- Parrots that are being converted from seed – only diet to other types of diet. Parrots should be initially offered with Harrison's High Potency diet for at least 6 months to make the diet switch effective.

Chapter Three: Acquiring, Feeding & Housing Poicephalus Parrots

- It's perfect for parrots who are overweight/ underweight, those that are molting, birds that are very active, those that are located in cold climate, birds that are in the recovery period, or parrots that has kidney/ liver disease.

- If your bird is weaning, you should offer Harrison's High Potency Formula diet for around 6 to 9 months.

- If your parrot is breeding, you must feed your females with this diet for 1 to 2 months before the breeding period, and until the chicks are fully weaned.

- You can increase the amount of supplemental organic veggies and fruits until the baby birds are fully weaned.

Chapter Three: Acquiring, Feeding & Housing Poicephalus Parrots

Some birds will immediately eat this new diet, and some might be a little finicky. Here are some tips on how you can convert your Pet Poicephalus to Harrison's diet:

- You can purchase Harrison's Bird Bread Mix because this is an effective conversion tool. What you can do is to add the bread mix to the current diet of your parrot. Then slowly reduce the amount of the bread mix food, and replace it with Harrison's High Potency Formula diet.

- Gradually transition your bird from a seed – only diet to this formulated diet mix. What you can do in the evening is to offer seeds for only about an hour. Once you've done that, you can try and remove the seed mix and replace it with Harrison's High Potency formula. The following day (morning and night), provide your bird with seed diet again but this time for just 30 minutes before providing Harrison's brand. The following day reduced it for 15 minutes, and then fully offer Harrison's High Potency Formula the

Chapter Three: Acquiring, Feeding & Housing Poicephalus Parrots

whole day. Make sure to monitor your bird's droppings.

- You can also use a converted bird role model; what you can do is to house your pet near another bird that's already eating Harrison's brands. This is what experts call as 'trainer bird' or a role model as parrots often copy other birds if they are eating a certain type of diet.

- Another thing you can do is heat up and moistens the food using a small amount of fruit juice to make it enticing for your pet bird.

- If the conversion tips don't work the first time, what you can do is to be patient and just keep on trying (at least 3 attempts). Feeding your bird with this kind of diet is worthwhile for your bird's long – term health.

Chapter Three: Acquiring, Feeding & Housing Poicephalus Parrots

- Your pet's body condition, behavior, and feces should be carefully monitored every day or at least a few times a week to see if your bird is successfully transitioning in its diet.

When it comes to supplementation, it shouldn't be more than 10% of your bird's overall diet. Do not add non – essential vitamins or fillers like other animal food products. You can also feed your bird with organic veggies and fruits in just small quantities like the following:

- Dark green leafy veggies
- Parsley
- Carrots
- Winter squash
- Pumpkin
- Sweet potatoes
- Mango
- Papaya
- Broccoli

Chapter Three: Acquiring, Feeding & Housing Poicephalus Parrots

Here are some of the other important ingredients of this formulated diet:

- Hulled Gray Millet
- Hull-less Barley
- Corn
- Toasted Soybeans
- Peanut Kernels
- Sunflower Kernels
- Peas
- Lentils
- Toasted Oat Groats
- Brown Rice
- Chia
- Alfalfa

#5: **Higgins Mayan Harvest Blends for Parrots**

The Higgins Mayan Harvest Blends for Parrots inspired by ancient cultures of South and Central America. Mayan Harvest diet is a combination of healthy parrot

Chapter Three: Acquiring, Feeding & Housing Poicephalus Parrots

nutrition and 'holistic wisdom' since this is inspired by the diet of native tropical birds that ancient cultures consider as sacred back then.

The Higgins Mayan Harvest has a balance mix of gourmet seed blends, veggies, nuts, legumes, exotic herbs, naturally – dehydrated fruits, and spices. All mixes are excellent for your parrot's overall health because it's also dusted with bee pollen. It's free of preservatives, and artificial colors. There are two kinds of delicious blends by the name of Tikal, and Celestial to accommodate your bird's varied diet. It's suitable for Senegal Poicephalus species, Amazon parrots, Macaws, hookbills, and also Cockatoos. Here are some of the important ingredients of the 2 blends:

Tikal Blend

- Shelled Almonds
- Roasted Soybean
- Fried green peas
- Safflower

Chapter Three: Acquiring, Feeding & Housing Poicephalus Parrots

- Sunflower seed
- Pumpkin seed
- Cantaloupe
- Hot chili peppers
- Sweet potatoes
- Cranberries
- Coconut chips
- Juniper berries
- Hulled oats
- Blueberries
- Buckwheat
- Hemp seed
- Chamomile flowers
- Beets
- Cashews

Celestial Blend

- Shelled peanuts
- Apples
- Whole apricots

Chapter Three: Acquiring, Feeding & Housing Poicephalus Parrots

- Safflower seed
- Rasted soybean
- Sunflower kernels
- Brazil nuts
- Sweet peppers
- Roasted green split peas
- Cherries
- Pineapple
- Kafir
- Spring wheat
- Flaked carrot
- Cinnamon sticks
- Pepitas
- Black beans
- Kidney beans
- Roasted garbanzo
- Shelled filberts
- Rosemary

Chapter Three: Acquiring, Feeding & Housing Poicephalus Parrots

Feeding Directions

You should fill the food bowl with as much food and it must be eaten within the 24 hour period. The ideal measurement is ½ to ¾ cups for larger Poicephalus species, and 1 to ½ cup for smaller Poicephalus species. Consult your vet first to make sure that you are feeding the right amount for your pet.

- Higgin's Tikal Blend contains around 12% of Crude Protein, 13% Crude Fat, 9% Crude Fiber, and 11.50% Moisture.

- Higgin's Celestial Blend contains around 12.25% of Crude Protein, 16% Crude Fat, 9.20% Crude Fiber, and 12% Moisture.

Hand – Feeding Your Parrot

When you hand feed your bird for the first time, you want to make sure that you're calm, slow, and also quite entertaining. You can do this by communicating with them

Chapter Three: Acquiring, Feeding & Housing Poicephalus Parrots

or interacting with them while you're hand is around the cage. Focus on both verbal and physical interaction.

What you need to do is to remove the food bowls for at least an hour during the day and at night so that they are quite hungry. Place the food on your palm, and have the grains on your hand while slowly placing your hand inside its cage.

Never offer the food directly to your bird or get your palm anywhere near them. Just place it inside the cage with about 30 cm distance, and let the parrot naturally come to you. You can do this for about three days for at least half an hour each morning and night. Don't move your palm too much because your parrot might get scared, just keep it steady until your pet comes and eats from your hand.

Your bird will eventually get used to your hand feeding, and once that happens, you can now add a unique command each time you hand feed them. This will alert your Poicephalus parrot that you will open the cage, and will hand feed them. Some birds tend to forget the whole thing which is why it's important to repeat the process every

Chapter Three: Acquiring, Feeding & Housing Poicephalus Parrots

day and be very consistent with what you do so that they'll remember it and treat it as part of their routine.

Setting a feeding time for your bird, doing the same gestures, and saying the same commands is recommended throughout your pet's lifetime because they'll easily remember and learn this way.

Chapter Four: Grooming Tips for Your Poicephalus Parrots

Grooming your pet parrot is a part of your bird's hygiene, and it's also a great way to strengthen your bond with him/ her. Grooming includes not just bathing your bird but also making sure that its beak is healthy and strong, its wings are finely clip, and its nails are also cut to ensure that it can maintain its balance, and avoid causing injuries to you once you take him/ her out of the cage. This chapter will guide you on how you can properly groom your pet Poicephalus to maintain a healthy lifestyle.

Chapter Four: Grooming Tips for Your Poicephalus Parrots

Grooming Your Poicephalus Parrots

Poicephalus parrots love to languish under a mild 'shower' in its natural habitat whenever there's a rain. Your main goal when it comes to grooming is to at least attempt in mimicking the bird's natural environment so that your parrot wouldn't be shock in your attempt to clean him/ her.

One of the best things to do is to go online or ask the breeder where you bought your parrot from because these people will give you the advantage of finding out what worked for them, and they may be able to answer any grooming questions that you may have. As with anything else, your Poicephalus parrot have their own set of behavior and habits, their grooming attitude is no different. Make sure to take the time to observe your pet once you groom them to see how they will react to certain things because some parrots are afraid of 'grooming time.'

Chapter Four: Grooming Tips for Your Poicephalus Parrots

Cleaning Your Parrot

Misting or spraying the feathers of your pet is very good to maintain skin and plumage conditions. It is a crucial part of the personal hygiene of your pet Poicephalus. In the wild, birds cherish the rain and some of them would even lie on its back or flap their wings because this is the only time that they can clean themselves naturally.

What you can do to bathe your parrot is to use either a good spray head or a hand held shower sprayer. Set the temperature to lukewarm and mist their body. Do not spray it directly on their eyes. Another thing you can do is to bring your parrot with you while you're showering and let him/her stand in a strong perch or in a safe place, and let your bird get misted from your shower. Make sure to supervise your pet if you're going to do this.

Chapter Four: Grooming Tips for Your Poicephalus Parrots

Clipping the Wings

The most important thing you need to remember is to you don't want to clip a baby parrots wings as it will need time to learn how to use them. Follow the tips below:

Trim the wings of the parrot.

Clipping the wings must be done in a regular basis especially if you prefer in discouraging your parrot from taking flight. Make sure that you do this routinely to prevent your pet flying out and losing it. However, make sure to not clip too much otherwise it could result in your Poicephalus parrot crashing down because of its inability to take proper flight; this will of course result in an injury.

Decide if you will let your parrot fly around the house or if you will completely discourage it.

There are many conflicting opinions about whether to clip or not to clip a parrot's wings. Allowing your bird to fly around the house can knock over things, and may get your bird into hazardous situations. It may lose its feathers or may even

Chapter Four: Grooming Tips for Your Poicephalus Parrots

escape. Another thing that keepers consider is the fact that birds are design to fly so why would you take away this skill by clipping the wings? Consider this fact and answer that question.

Ask the help of professionals.

You can ask your vet or your breeder for any recommendations as to how much you need to clip your parrot's wings. When you do decide to clip your parrot's wings, it's probably best that you employ the services of a professional before attempting to do it on your own.

Supervise your parrot's flights

Consider using a clicker to train your parrot to return to you if you do decide to train them to fly. The key is supervising them and training them to come back to you. You can also use a clicker to avert naughty behavior from your parrot. Consider hiring a parrot trainer or attend a formal bird training session so that you can learn how to train your parrot especially when it comes to supervised flying.

Chapter Four: Grooming Tips for Your Poicephalus Parrots

Keeping the Beak Healthy

Trim your parrot's beak.

If the parrot's beak becomes overgrown or deformed it then needs to be trimmed. There are a lot of items to help your Poicephalus parrot keep its beak in shape and some of these materials can be easily bought at your local pet stores or online pet stores. You can purchase grooming materials like lava blocks, mineral blocks, and other beak grooming items. All these materials can be helpful in smoothing your parrot's beaks.

Learn how to properly file your parrot's beak.

If you choose to do it by yourself, just be careful because you don't want to file too much otherwise you'll end up injuring your parrot. Ask an expert to make a demo to you so that you can learn the techniques of how to carry out the procedure before doing it yourself.

Chapter Four: Grooming Tips for Your Poicephalus Parrots

Trimming the Nails

Trim the overgrown nails.

The main purpose of your parrot's nails is to keep a hold of the perch and keep its balance but if the nails of your parrot becomes too long this may prevent your bird from perching properly. Overgrown nails could also cause it to unintentionally scratch you as well.

Learn how to properly clip your parrot's nails.

There are various concrete perches available at pet shops or online that would help keep the nails of your parrot trimmed. You may want to also invest on a good pair of clippers. If you're going to do it yourself, make sure to ask take advice from an expert or just let your vet do it for you. Keep in mind that the quick grows along with the nail, if you accidentally cut this part, it will deeply hurt your parrot so make sure that you have a styptic powder to aid the bleeding just in case.

Chapter Four: Grooming Tips for Your Poicephalus Parrots

Chapter Five: Forming a Bond with Your Poicephalus Parrots

This chapter will give you tips on how you can handle your pet once it arrives. Properly handling them on their first few days will kick – start your relationship with your pet. Once you've successfully done that, forming a bond with them will be much easier. You can eventually progress to other training them, and also doing basic tricks. Building trust is the key in your relationship with your bird; your pet must treat you as part of its flock. This is the only

Chapter Five: Forming a Bond with Your Poicephalus Parrot

way to make a meaningful connection to them. Gaining your pet's trust is worthwhile because if they already treat you as a family, they'll easily follow you. This will come naturally so don't rush the training process.

Tips in Gaining Your Bird's Trust

The following points are very important if you want to let your parrot trust you. As they say, first impression lasts; this is true for animals in general. Do not make the mistake of other newbie keepers otherwise it'll be difficult for you to form a bond with your Poicephalus parrot. Follow the suggested tips below and adjust accordingly:

Find a good cage location.

Tip#1: Find a good location in your house for your bird's cage. Make sure that there's enough foot traffic, and never isolate them otherwise they'll never get use to people around. Exposing them to the members of the family is a good way to let them know that they are welcome in the new environment.

Chapter Five: Forming a Bond with Your Poicephalus Parrot

Tip#2: Find a safe training spot. Your house should be parrot – proof. It has to be safe if in case you want to let your bird out for training. You don't want to train them in areas where they are near hazardous objects or your other household pets that can potentially injure or scare them.

Tip#3: Keep the room/ house secured. Make sure that the room is also secured to prevent your bird from escaping or flying away once you let them out of the cage. Poicephalus parrots are smart creatures with a good flight skill. If you're a newbie keeper, it'll be hard for you to get them back. The last thing you want to do is to go after your bird because they may mistake you as a predator.

Let your parrot settle in its new house or environment
Tip#1: Leave your parrot alone (at least for the first few days). Make sure that you provide your pet with fresh food and water after you make the transition to its permanent cage. Once you do that, the most important tip is to let your parrot settle and just leave them be.

Chapter Five: Forming a Bond with Your Poicephalus Parrot

Tip#2: Allow it to adjust to its new cage, to its new environment, and to you. Don't handle it for the next few days or so, just provide food and water on its cage. Do a 'hands – off' interaction with them. Most parrots in general will need some time to adjust to its new surroundings. It will be tempting for you to touch and interact with your pet bird but keep in mind that they're still not familiar with you so it's better to introduce yourself slowly.

Tip#3: Take note of their behavior. Most new birds will spend some time at the bottom of its cage. This is normal parrot behavior so don't panic. Poicephalus parrots fear change; they could be anxious about its new environment so just monitor them every now and then until they become familiar with their new surroundings. It'll probably take around a few days to a few weeks depending on your pet's personality. Some birds are more social than others, just avoid handling him/ her but still interact with it.

Chapter Five: Forming a Bond with Your Poicephalus Parrot

Form a bond with your pet bird through interaction and 'hands – off' activities.

Tip#1: You can interact with your bird through a non – physical interaction. An example of that is sitting in front of the cage and simply communicating with them every day. Again never attempt to touch or handle your bird for the first few days or weeks. Provide your pet with toys, and perches, and make sure to talk to your bird so that it can get use to your voice, tone, and your actions.

Tip #2: Let other family members or housemates (if any) communicate with your pet from time to time. If ever more than one person wants to train your pet or interact with it, then it's best that both of you sit down together and communicate with the bird. However, make sure that you don't also crowd up the bird because you'll most probably scare it off. Too much noise and people will overwhelm them and might make them stress.

Chapter Five: Forming a Bond with Your Poicephalus Parrot

Tip #3: Speak to it in a calm and soothing manner and call your pet by name. This will make your pet eventually recognize you and feel comfortable around you. You can also start calling it by its name, and talk to it every time you come home from work or whenever you'll leave the house so that it'll know that you are referring to him/ her with that name.

Handling Proper

Tip #1: Let your bird know you're there and let him/ her get comfortable with you. The first thing to do after your newfound pet has finally settled down is to start handling them. However, this should be done slowly. What you can do is to sit down in front of the cage while slowly placing your hand on one side of the cage. Try to do this every day for a consecutive of three days; at least one hour during the day, and one hour at night. After doing that for about three days, you can then place your hand on all sides of the cage and follow the same instructions. This is done so that your bird will not get shock or feel traumatized once you've finally tried and reach out your hand inside the cage.

Chapter Five: Forming a Bond with Your Poicephalus Parrot

Tip #2: See your bird's reactions and take it slow if need be. The goal is to start seeing that your bird is beginning to adapt to your hand, and recognize it as a moving object that can be seen outside the bird cage. What you need to achieve at this stage is to see your parrot drink or eat their food while your hand is placed on the cage. This is a sign that your Poicephalus parrot is already comfortable with you. If that's not the case yet, then adjust accordingly. See if your bird is handling this well, and if you think they're still not ready, give it time to adjust. Be extra patient.

Tip #3: Open the door of the cage and slowly place your hand inside. Once you've noticed that your pet doesn't mind your hand being placed outside of its cage, you can try the next step which is to open the door, and then place your hand inside. Put your hand on the left side of the cage for three days, on the right side for another three days, then on the top and bottom for the next few days. What we're trying to do here is to make your hand a subset of the comfort zone. This stage becomes quite tricky for some people because they usually rush this process. Don't touch your bird at this

Chapter Five: Forming a Bond with Your Poicephalus Parrot

stage because it will still be scary for them if you do. Not touching them at this point is crucial because it will make your parrot really trust you. What you're simply doing is introducing yourself to them – this is quite tedious but it can also be a rewarding experience for you and your pet.

Training Proper

Tip #1: Slow and steady always does the trick when it comes to training a Poicephalus parrot. Like any other pet, you should let your parrot grow accustomed to your voice, your presence and its new environment when it arrives home. After giving your pet a few days to be comfortable around you, you can proceed to teaching them basic parrot training. If you get to a handfed baby Poicephalus, you won't have much trouble handling it as it is already used to human care.

Tip#2: Set a training schedule and limit your sessions. Most parrots are receptive to training at night so take note of that because Poicephalus parrots are not different. Make

Chapter Five: Forming a Bond with Your Poicephalus Parrot

sure that you also limit your sessions to less than 30 minutes and have about 1 hour interval before you begin a new session.

Tip#3: Reward your pet during your training. Your first session can be to get your Poicephalus parrot to receive a treat from you. When it does, you can gently scratch its head as a reward. This is equivalent to gaining trust. Once you've fully handled them already, you can move on to other things such as teaching them to step on your hand. The length of this initial training depends on the kind of bird you get. If it is a hand - fed chick, it will be immediate but if it's an untamed older bird accepting a treat and training can take longer than expected.

Tip#4: Teach your bird some cool tricks like stepping up, standing on your finger, and mimicking human sounds. Stepping – up is one of the basics of bird training. What you need to do is to approach your pet with your hand with the food. Once it does, do not move, just be still, and let your

Chapter Five: Forming a Bond with Your Poicephalus Parrot

parrot eat the treats in your palm. This is a positive reinforcement to get your pet to step up in your hand, and build trust. Repeat this process for more than a week. Once your Poicephalus parrot trusts you and is no longer shy around you, you can train its behavior and teach it new tricks. As with any pet training, you need to remember that frequency of sessions and repetition of activities are vital. Your Poicephalus parrot can mimic most sounds but they learn environmental sounds faster and better than human voices. Don't be frustrated when your Poicephalus cannot mimic as many human words compared to other parrot species.

Tip #5: Never ever punishes your Poicephalus parrot! You will effectively destroy whatever trust you've built with your bird when you do so, and you will not get it to follow you or learn anything else. Still do the basics like placing your hand inside the cage, conversing with it, hand feeding it without imposing to touch it, and commanding it to step – up. Do not change anything, follow your routine, say the

Chapter Five: Forming a Bond with Your Poicephalus Parrot

same commands, do the same gestures, and just add this one routine.

Tip #6: Play and exercise are activities important for the psychological health and physical well - being of your Poicephalus parrot. They are active by nature so be sure to provide your pet with a lot of exercise equipment fit for them. Otherwise they may become overweight and if they do they will become sedentary birds. Activities also help prevent problems and deter stress like screeching. Give your parrot lots of fun activities to keep it occupied, such as bird ladders, ropes, chains, parrot swings, fresh branches to gnaw and chew, and remember to switch it up with new bird toys on a regular basis.

Taming Your Poicephalus Parrot

Once your pet Poicephalus has already gotten used to the different routines, you can now start teaching it other tricks. You can continue using the step – up technique or ladder technique using your finger, and rewarding it with

Chapter Five: Forming a Bond with Your Poicephalus Parrot

treats using your palm. You can then start asking them to step – up on your shoulders from your hand, and then offer a reward. Repeat the trick over and over every time you do training twice a day until it's locked in their memory. Don't rush and be patient.

Once you've done all the basics keep in mind the following taming techniques in case your parrot experiences some form of unwanted behavior:

Exercise control over your Poicephalus parrot.

When Poicephalus parrots are younger, you might feel that they are safe whenever they climb over you or while you let them on your shoulder but when they grow larger, and become quite aggressive, you need to be more careful and pay close attention because they can try to escape from you. The best way to establish basic control over your Poicephalus parrot is through positive reinforcement, and you can do that by commanding your bird to step up or down, or other basic commands you already taught. You can also spend time with your bird while it's on the cage by

Chapter Five: Forming a Bond with Your Poicephalus Parrot

bringing it near you when you're doing household chores to keep him/ her occupied.

Exercise situational awareness whenever you're handling your parrot.

If you don't pay attention to your Poicephalus parrot he/ she will tend to become out of control especially when you take him/ her out of the cage. He/ she might try to climb over you, peck you a bit, or fly away from you. If ever your pet persist this kind of naughty behavior put him / her back down to its cage and try again after a few minutes to let your bird know that it's an unacceptable behavior.

Minimize your parrot's breeding instincts.

If you don't want any unwanted pregnancies or issues of territoriality. You must remove potential nesting materials. It's quite instinctive for birds in general to feel protective of a certain space if they see things where they can potentially nest in. Minimizing your parrot's breeding

Chapter Five: Forming a Bond with Your Poicephalus Parrot

instincts will prevent issues of territoriality especially if you have more than one bird in a cage.

Maintain your composure if ever they tried to bite you.

There could be a point where your Poicephalus parrot will become quite naughty, and may try to bite you especially when you are trying to pet them or hand – feed them. The most important thing you need to do is to not let your parrot see a negative response from you. Don't scream or scare it off by slapping its cage to show your frustration. Just place it back to its cage and talk to it the way you will scold a child but in a mannered way so that your parrot will not develop any aggressive behavior. It's also important that you don't let your bird hear angry shouts or screams from you/ your family members to reduce the likelihood of being scared or aggression.

Chapter Six: Pairing Poicephalus

Your parrot's body language and behavior becomes quite different when they are paired with just one species compared to pairing it up with 2 or more species pairs. The parrots tend to also act differently in terms of sexual behavior when they know that someone (like their owners) is watching them. Part of the courting or mating process is foreplay – just like in humans. You may see the birds you paired up to be perching together in one twig, or foraging on the same nut, these are good signs that they are compatible with one another. If you notice that they both act busy, or

Chapter Six: Pairing Poicephalus

one parrot tries to keep stay away from the other by flying away if one makes a 'move,' then they're not compatible.

If you notice these subtle signs for about a day or so, it's probably best that you separate them, and find another pair for your Poicephalus bird especially if they become aggressive because they might try to eventually kill one another because of territorial issues since they prefer not to share it together. This chapter will guide you on how you can breed your Poicephalus birds should you choose to become one. It's very important to learn how these parrots react and behave whenever you're trying to breed them so that you can do it properly and safely.

Bonded Pairs vs. Compatible Pairs

Bonded is not synonymous to compatibility. There are many parrot breeders out there who might sell you with 'bonded pairs' of parrots but it doesn't necessarily mean that these birds like each other, and it's also not good for breeding. In fact, two parrots of the same sex can be bonded; you might be expecting an offspring from these bonded

Chapter Six: Pairing Poicephalus

pairs, only to find out that they cannot reproduce. It's best to have your Poicephalus parrots' DNA tested to know if you have a male and female.

Birds can be bonded but can still be incompatible. Bonded pairs have one dominant and submissive bird making it quite stressful for the submissive one. You don't want to stress your pet if in case he/she turns out to be the submissive one so make sure that only pair up parrots that are compatible with one another.

The question is how will you know if they are compatible with one another? You have to sort of sneak in on them to see how they behave towards each other – when you're not around. Parrots usually act quite different when they can sense your presence which is why it's best if you just give them some time by themselves and sort of creep in every now and then to see if they really have that connection even if no one is watching them.

Chapter Six: Pairing Poicephalus

Courting and Mating

Once you've determined that the Poicephalus parrots you paired up are compatible and have some form of affectionate mutual connection, you can expect that there will be some form of courtship between the two. Each parrot species has some form of ritual if they are interested in mating or copulating, so just give them time to do that. Courtship may take a few minutes to a few days after you've placed them in a cage.

When it comes to the copulation process, the male sometimes mounts the female but sometimes it's the other way around. The mating lasts for just a couple of minutes but it can take as long as around 15 to 20 minutes. It's usually slow and deliberate. The mating process may go for a few days to a month before you see any eggs being laid.

Chapter Six: Pairing Poicephalus

Egg Laying and Nesting

Usually Poicephalus parrots particularly the Senegals and the Meyer's aren't serious about nesting until after the hen laid the 2nd or 3rd egg. It will take about 28 days (the incubation period) after the first egg is laid before it hatches.

Now here's the most important part, as the breeder, it's your job to constantly check the newly hatched chicks and at some point you have to pull them out of the nest (at least around 3 weeks) to wean them out. Before you wean the babies out of their parent's side, you have to do it with caution because some pairs panic when they feel that someone is threatening their young. Some pairs however, are more open to their owners touching their young.

Nesting and Territorial Issues

If you plan on checking the babies out, it's best that you let the parents know that you're around through tapping the nesting box first or the cage before your hands reach inside to avoid panic. There are many instances where

Chapter Six: Pairing Poicephalus

the parents kill their chicks or abandon them because they feel that they are being threatened.

Territoriality is a big issue for most bird species, and if they feel like their privacy is being compromised, the natural instinct of these birds is to defend their territory, and kill their chicks as they wouldn't want to raise their young in a place that's not "safe." If security is not met, they will ultimately abandon or kill their young because the parents must feel secure in the space that they are in. It's their job to protect the babies, and no one including you, their keeper, will get their chicks. They will fight to the death if they have to.

If ever the pairs are housed with another pairs or other bird species in the same aviary for instance, it's best that you put up a divider or some form of partitions between the cages to avoid territorial issues. Senegal Poicephalus species and Meyer's Poicephalus parrots are the most vicious when it comes to defending their nest and territories to their neighbors. The Red – Bellied Poicephalus will bicker and breed, while the Jardine Poicephalus will not really care about other birds or threats while they are nesting until the eggs hatch – they go crazy in keeping you and the other birds away from their chicks. Cape Poicephalus parrots are also territorial much like Amazon birds even if they're not brooding.

Signs of Sexual Maturity

The Senegal, Meyer's, Jardine's, and Brown – headed Poicephalus species reaches sexual maturity when they reach one year of age. The eye color of Poicephalus species is not really an indicator of age as compared to what most people say because 3 month old species like Red – Bellies, Meyer's and Senegal parrots already have the same eye color as an adult species but it changes when these birds go outside.

Chapter Six: Pairing Poicephalus

Chapter Seven: Raising Poicephalus Chicks

Perhaps one of the most difficult jobs in the world is to become a parent. This is true with animals including parrots. It's also an endearing characteristic that a breeder like you is happy to take this kind of endeavor, of being a second 'parent' to the offspring of your Poicephalus pet. Rearing baby Poicephalus parrots is a whole new level because this time, you are caring for a more delicate species. If you think putting up with your Poicephalus parrot is already difficult, what more for baby birds? You will need to provide twice the effort, time, and attention to keep these newborn chicks healthy and safe. Raising chicks will require you to go beyond what you know about keeping a parrot, it can be a huge responsibility especially if you choose to become a reputable breeder but it's definitely an endeavor worth doing. This chapter will give you an overview of what you can expect in raising chicks and becoming a breeder.

Parenting

When it comes to Poicephalus species, not all of them are quite good in parenting which is why the responsibility somehow falls on you as their keeper.

Usually, a first time mom or hen is more protective than when she already laid clutch a second time. If it's your pet's first egg laying experience, try not to disturb her too much as she may mistake you for invading her privacy or threatening the chicks. You may find your bird constantly with her eggs until it hatches; she'll also spend so much time in the nest box and may never come out for quite some time. What you can do is to just check in on them once in a while to make sure that everything's okay inside the nest box but don't

Chapter Seven: Raising Poicephalus Chicks

bother them all the time as the mom could panic and might end up mutilating the chicks due to security threat.

As your female pet becomes a seasoned breeder, she will be more relaxed, and may probably be more welcoming of you. She may allow you to check in on her eggs and babies without getting nervous but it's still best if you make the parents aware that you will be checking them out prior to you opening the cage or the nest box. As mentioned earlier, your presence can be known by tapping the cage three times before reaching in.

Some Poicephalus parent parrots leave the nest a few days prior to hatching. Some hen keeps warming the eggs until it hatches. Whatever the trick is, it's best to just leave them be, and perhaps just pull the eggs out for incubation around 3 weeks after being laid.

Chapter Seven: Raising Poicephalus Chicks

Pulling Chicks

Pulling out chicks from their parents can be both traumatic for the babies and the hen. Some baby chicks tend to have a sweet kind of temperament prior to pulling but once pulled, some of them changes temperament. How you pull out the chicks from their moms and dads could greatly affect the personality of these young chicks so make sure that you do it right, and pull them out carefully so that hand – rearing as well as hand – feeding the chicks can be successful and "trauma – free."

Sibling Aggression

Poicephalus parrots seem to have a natural aggressive behavior towards their siblings. The Jardine's is the worst when it comes to sibling rivalries, while the Meyer's parrots come next. Red – bellied Poicephalus as well as Senegals don't hate their siblings as much.

You have to understand that even if you give these baby birds the same level of care, it doesn't mean that they

Chapter Seven: Raising Poicephalus Chicks

will have the same set of behaviors or personality especially towards one another. Some chicks will grow up to be nippier or more skittish than the others – and that's okay. However, the problem begins when they start pecking at one another as it would cause injuries in the long run, and you can't really do anything about it. If you have a brother or sister growing up, you will understand that this is just a way of life.

What some keepers found out is that when they had the baby chicks sexed, it's usually the clutches with an uneven balance of sexes that experiences sibling aggression. If a clutch has more females than males, the males will get picked on, and vice – versa. If this is the case, you may want to separate them up as they grow a little older to avoid any extreme forms of aggression to one another.

Keep in Mind!

The most important thing to keep in mind especially when it comes to keeping parrots, and raising chicks is to pay attention to subtle things – your birds' behaviors, and reactions will tell you what they like and don't like or how

Chapter Seven: Raising Poicephalus Chicks

they want things to be done. Make sure that you hear them out so that you won't just be a responsible breeder but more of a second parent to them.

Glossary of Important Terms

Addled eggs - These eggs are not viable and will not hatch.

Afterfeather - A structure that projects from the shaft of the feather at the rim of the superior umbilicus.

Allopreening - An act of social grooming amongst birds, in which one bird preens the other or a pair of birds does so mutually.

alternate plumage - The plumage of birds displayed in time for courtship or a breeding season.

Altricial - hatchlings with their eyes closed, and are not capable of leaving the nest on its own, and relies on parents for food.

Alula - a bird's "thumb"

Anisodactylus - a bird foot which has three toes pointing forward and one toe pointing at the back

Anting - a behaviour when birds rub insects, typically ants, on their feathers and skin

Aviculture - captive breeding and raising of birds

Back- exterior area of a bird's upper parts between its mantle and rump

basic plumage - non-breeding plumage

Beak - bill or rostrum

beak trimming - the partial removal of the beak

Belly - the area beneath the chest of a bird

Billing - a tendency of mated pairs that strengthen couple bonding

bird banding - a tag attached to the leg of a bird to enable identification

bird strike - bird/s that impact with planes in flight

Body down - soft, down feathers underneath a birds outer feathers.

Breast - body part between throat and belly

breeding plumage - plumage displayed by birds during breeding season

Brood - offspring birds

brood patch - an area of bare skin well supplied with blood vessels at the surface, and facilitates the transfer of heat to the eggs

Call - bird vocalization intending to serve as warning alarm

Cloaca - birds expel waste from it; other mate by joining cloaca; females lay eggs from this region

contact call - to make known to their kind the location of a bird

Crissum - feathered area between the vent and the tail

cryptic plumage - plumage meant to camouflage birds

definitive plumage - plumage completely developed and fixed

Down - the softest of the birds feathers

Egg - where birds develop until hatched

egg incubation - act of warming the eggs to promote hatching

Eye-ring - visible ring of feathers surrounding a bird's eyes

Feather - distinct outer "garment" covering a birds' body

feather pecking - a behavioural problem when one bird repeatedly pecks at the feathers of another bird

Fledge - a young bird that completely develops its wing muscles and feather suitable for flight

Fledgling - the period when a completely formed young bird ventures out of the nest and learns to take flight

Flight - the act of soaring in the air with the use of wings

Gizzard - specialized stomach organ found in the digestive tract of some birds used to grind up food and aided with grit or stone particles

Gleaning - a bird strategy used to catch insect prey

Grooming - the act of preening and self-cleaning

Iris - coloured outer ring surrounding birds' pupil

Lek - male aggression when in competition for the attention of a female

Mantle - front area of a bird's upper portion found between nape and top back

Migration - seasonal movement of birds

Morph - a polymorphic plumage colour variance between the same species

Moult - a periodic shedding and replacement of feathers

Nail - hard tissue at the tip of a bird's beak

Nares - two holes leading to the nasal cavities in the bird's skull

Nest - a bird's lair and home; where a female lays eggs and roosts

Over-brooding - a phenomenon when birds continue to brood eggs not likely to hatch

Passerine - any bird of the order Passeriformes

Pinioning - the removal of the joint of a bird's wing farthest from the body preventing flight

Plumage - refers to feathers covering a bird as well as pattern, colour and arrangement of feathers

Plumeology - the study of feathers

pre-alternate moult - also known as the prenuptial moult when basic plumage is shed to make way for nuptial plumage

prebasic moult - moult birds go through after breeding season

Precocial - young birds that after hatched has their eyes open

Preening - grooming od feathers in birds

Quill - the main stem of a feather where all structures branch from

Resident - a non-migratory bird

rictal bristles stiff, tapering feathers around the eyes of some birds

Rosette - a found at the corners of the beaks of some birds. A fleshy rosette area

Rump - area of a bird's body between the end of the back and the base of the tail

sexual dimorphism - common occurrence amongst birds in which males and females of a similar sort display different character traits

Song - bird vocalization associated with courtship

Speculum - A patch of typically bright coloured feathers, often iridescent

Sternum - bird's breastbone

Syrinx - the vocal organs of birds

Tail streamers - narrow tips of the tail of some birds

Talon - claw of bird of prey

Teleoptiles - feathers of an adult bird

Throat - body area located between the chin and the upper part of the breast

Thigh - body part between knee and trunk of the bird's body

Vent - the outer opening of the cloaca

Wings - The bird's forelimbs that are the essential to flight

Wingspan - distance between wings from one wing tip to the other

Photo Credits

Page Photo by user Allan Hopkins via Flickr.com,

https://www.flickr.com/photos/hoppy1951/16108874158/

Page Photo by user Allan Hopkins via Flickr.com,

https://www.flickr.com/photos/hoppy1951/34614226652/

Page Photo by user Bram Cymet via Flickr.com,

https://www.flickr.com/photos/bcymet/6102472879/

Page Photo by user Bram Cymet via Flickr.com,

https://www.flickr.com/photos/bcymet/3284144053/

Page Photo by user Bram Cymet via Flickr.com,

https://www.flickr.com/photos/bcymet/6200418782/

Page Photo by user Bernard Dupont via Flickr.com,

https://www.flickr.com/photos/berniedup/6018229800/

Page Photo by user Bram Cymet via Flickr.com,

https://www.flickr.com/photos/bcymet/7304039626/

Page Photo by user Bram Cymet via Flickr.com,

https://www.flickr.com/photos/bcymet/7036215165/

References

"Poicephalus" – Wikipedia.org

https://en.wikipedia.org/wiki/Poicephalus

"Poicephalus" – Lafeber.com

https://lafeber.com/pet-birds/species/poicephalus/

"The Poicephalus Parrots" – AllPetBirds.com

http://www.allpetbirds.com/poicephalus

"Poicephalus: Short – Tailed Parrots" – BeautyofBirds.com

https://www.beautyofbirds.com/poicephalusinfo.htm

"4 Reasons Why *Poicephalus* Parrots Make Great Family Pets" – Petcha.com

https://www.petcha.com/4-reasons-why-poicephalus-parrots-make-great-family-pets/

"Poicephalus" – Goodbirdinc.com

http://www.goodbirdinc.com/parrot-profiles-poicephalus.html

"Poicephalus Parrots" – AvalonAviary.com

http://avalonaviary.com/poicephalus-parrots.aspx

"Senegal, Meyer's and other Poicephalus Parrots – Small Size but Large Rewards" – ThatPetPlace.com

http://blogs.thatpetplace.com/thatbirdblog/2010/12/28/senegal-meyers-and-other-poicephalus-parrots-small-size-but-large-rewards/#.W0eQqzpKi1s

"Breeding Poicephalus" – OldWorldAviaries.com

http://www.oldworldaviaries.com/text/miscellaneous/breed-poi.htm

www.ingramcontent.com/pod-product-compliance
Lightning Source LLC
Chambersburg PA
CBHW060838050426
42453CB00008B/734